Hello Children

by Shirley Salmon

A collection of songs and related
activities for children aged 4–9

With original drawings by Helga Wilberg

SMC 572

SCHOTT

Mainz • London • Madrid • New York • Paris • Prague • Tokyo • Toronto

SMC 572

ISMN M-60001-045-5
UPC   841886008786
ISBN   978-1-84761-052-2

Design, typesetting and music engraving by William Holab

Contents

Introduction

There is a multitude of ideas hidden in most children's playsongs whether these are found in song books or learned and passed down on the playground. These ideas are not only musical but often include opportunities to extend language, concepts, movement, coordination, cooperation, and imagination. They provide a wealth of opportunities for singing, moving, playing, creating, and also learning. Play songs appeal to children and provide a means of learning through active involvement, especially through physical movement. The links between physical movement and intellectual development are large. Children who explore movements over and over again are in the process of working through a particular "form of thought" or concept. Play songs can not only help children develop concepts through movement, but they also encourage linguistic development in extending vocabulary and by experimenting with rhymes, rhythms, and repetition.

In this collection I want not only to pass on some wonderful songs and activities but also to include some of my ideas that have been inspired by them. I call these ideas "extensions" as they extend the original version of the song going into related areas and are useful impulses for children of different ages and abilities. The extensions can go into: sensory awareness, movement and dance, voice and language, playing instruments, listening, visualizing, social forms, and drama. Exploring many of these possibilities often needs many days or even weeks. As songs are often embedded in a topic or particular theme in the class, using extensions can lead to cross-curricular projects. Once a range of ideas has been developed then activities appropriate for the particular group and for the abilities of individual children can be chosen.

The book is written for preschool and primary teachers working with children aged 4–9, for music teachers, and for teachers working with groups of mixed ability. It aims to widen the repertoire of songs and related activities, to enhance the experience of singing, moving, and playing instruments together, as well as to stimulate the teacher's creativity to invent new extensions. Due to the wide range of tasks in the extensions it is possible to work on a song with a mainstream class ensuring that no one is over- or under-challenged and that each child can learn, play, and contribute to the whole on his or her own level. The accompaniments suggested should be thought of as models and, in the spirit of Carl Orff and Gunild Keetman, these should be modified and adapted according to the particular group. Songs are often full of images and can be the starting point for children to create their own drawings, paintings, poems, or stories. I hope those using this book will be as excited and stimulated as I have been in playing and singing these songs with many different groups, and the material will inspire teachers to follow new ideas for their children.

Extending Playsongs

Sensory Awareness
visual, auditory, tactile,
kinesthetic, vestibular

Movement   Voice/Language

Dance   Play Materials

                    The Theme /
Instruments   **The Playsong**   Social Forms

Listening   Drama

Visualizing   Related Subjects
e.g., notation forms,
visual arts

This page can be used like a mind-map to note down ideas stemming from a particular song or theme. Trying to find many ideas for each area can be very stimulating for the teacher. Connections between the different areas can also be seen and made. From this collection the teacher can select activities suitable to the abilities and needs of the particular class or group. Working from one theme or song can last over many weeks and can lead to other related subjects in the curriculum.

Children's activities can include:
perceiving, discovering, experimenting, playing, communicating, recognizing, remembering, imitating, varying, representing, presenting, discussing, deciding, inventing, practicing, forming, creating, performing, reflecting

Extending themes and playsongs to offer a wide range of experience

Playsongs can be the starting point for many types of activities. They can inspire us to broaden a specific theme while also emphasising particular concepts relevant for the group. Extensions may include, but are not limited to, the following:

Sensory Awareness: sight, sound, touch, vibration, kinaesthetics, balance

Movement: playful warm-up, movement experiment
Laban's basic body activities: locomotion, rotation, elevation, gesture, position
movement sequences, formations and paths
parameters: tempo, dynamics, form, space, accompaniment

Dance: preparatory exercises, traditional dance forms, popular dance forms, narrative dance, improvisation, composition

Voice & Language: breathing, posture, physical exercises
sounds, syllables, words, phrases
chants, rhymes, poems, story books

Play Materials: natural objects, toys
materials, e.g., scarves, balls, spinning tops
household objects, sounding objects, instruments

Instruments: body instruments, voice
sounding objects, elemental instruments
home-made instruments, classical instruments

Listening: sounds, noises, sounds of nature
live sounds, recorded sounds
sounds of voices, instruments
songs related to the topic, pieces of music related to the topic
poems or stories, different styles of music

Visualizing: in movement, on one's own body, with or for a partner
drawing, painting, working with clay
signs or symbols, forms of graphic notation
traditional notation

Social Forms: relationship play
playing individually, working next to or with a partner
working in a small group, working with the whole class
leading—following
communicating, cooperating

Drama: incorporating music, movement and language
reciting, pantomime, acting out the song
making props and costumes
using story books
elemental music drama

Recommended Reading

Athey, Chris, *Extending thought in young children: A parent-teacher partnership,* Paul Chapman Publishing Ltd., London, 2007.

Goodkin, Doug, *Play, sing and dance: An introduction to Orff-Schulwerk,* Schott, London, 2002.

Haselbach, Barbara, *Dance education: Basic principles and models for nursery and primary school,* Schott & Co. Ltd., London, 1978.

Haselbach, Barbara, *Improvisation, dance, movement,* Magnamusic-Baton, St. Louis, 1981.

Matterson, Elizabeth Mary (compiler), *This little puffin* [A classic treasury of nursery rhymes, songs and games], Penguin, London, 1999.

Mort, Linda, Jane Morris and Jane Bottomley, *Starting with rhyme,* Scholastic publications, Leamington Spa, UK, 1991.

Nordoff, Paul and Clive Robbins, *Children's playsongs,* Books 1–5, Theodore Presser Company, USA, 1962.

Nutbrown, Cathy, *Threads of Thinking: Young children learning and the role of early education.* Sage Publications Ltd., London, 2006.

Paynter, John and Peter Aston, *Sound and silence: Classroom projects in creative music,* Cambridge University Press, Cambridge, 1970.

Sherborne, Veronica, *Developmental movement for children: Mainstream, special needs and pre-school,* Worth Publishing, UK, 2001.

Acknowledgements

My first thanks go to Helga Wilberg who has enhanced the book with her beautiful drawings and whose drawing of Incy Wincy's web gave me the idea some years ago. To Carolee Stewart who was interested in the idea from the very beginning for including this book in the American Orff-Schulwerk supplements. Special thanks to my daughter Helen who over the years has brought home many interesting songs and games learned on various playgrounds and shared them with me. Thanks to Gerda Bächli for her inspiring work and wonderful songs and to Chris Athey for her interest, knowledge, and many stimulating discussions. I am grateful to Christoph Schartner for permission to use his melody ("My Friend") and to the publishers MusicVision, Switzerland for permission to use two songs by Gerda Bächli ("The Owl," "The Seasons"). Finally my thanks go to the many children, students, teachers, and colleagues who have sung and played these playsongs in their many different versions, contributed variations, and stimulated me to continue developing ideas.

Hello Children—Extensions

Sensory awareness
- Name one part of the body during the song, e.g., "Hello Hands," feel your hand; find different movements with your hands
- Choose other parts of the body and greet others, touching gently
- Choose one part of the body, move around the room and stick together with one or more partners (using this body part) at the end of the song
- Stay stuck and try to move without losing contact
- Encourage children to make suggestions
- Adapt the words using current classroom themes

Movement
- Explore movements with particular parts of the body
- Greet a particular shape, e.g., square, circle, line, triangle
- Find these in the classroom; draw them in the air or on the floor; make the shape with your body—alone or with a partner
- Let one child demonstrate and the others imitate
- Use patterns with body percussion to accompany

Language
- Name colors and let children wearing the color accompany with an instrument
- Name animals and use their individual sounds
- Name articles of clothing
- Name parts of the room and let children move there as quickly as possible
- Name furniture and let the children play the piece of furniture as an instrument
- Encourage the children to find new ideas
- Sing the song in different languages, e.g., German: "Hallo Kinder wir sind da (3X) Wir sind heute da."

Instruments
- Greet parts of the body and use them to accompany
- Greet different instruments, e.g., drum, triangle; listen to their distinctive sounds and use them to accompany the song
- Greet individual children: "Hello Peter how are you, how are you today"? Let the child improvise on a given or chosen instrument in answer to the question
- Use two congas (or other instruments) for a rondo: sing the song, greeting two children, then let the two children improvise – starting and finishing together

Hello Children

Text: Shirley Salmon

USA: Traditional

Hel - lo chil - dren we are here.
Hel - lo chil - dren we are here.
Hel - lo chil - dren we are here.
We are here to - day.

This is one of the most versatile songs I know, and it can be adapted for a wealth of activities. The melody is very similar to the well-known song "Skip to my Lou," and it appeals to all age groups. It is especially interesting for older children if the rhythm is syncopated. It doesn't necessarily need an accompaniment, but can be easily accompanied on the guitar.

Hey, Hello, Bonjour—Extensions

Voice/Language

- Find greetings in different languages
- Recite in unison or divide into groups
- Speak the words as a round
- Use parts of the song to build up ostinati
- Invent a goodbye verse, e.g., "Bye for now..."

Movement

- Find gestures for each greeting
- Find typical gestures from different countries
- Perform the gestures with and without the words
- Take one gesture and magnify the movement to move to a different spot
- Use magnified gestures (and their mirror images) to form a sequence
- Change one of the parameters (time / intensity / space) of a gesture

Instruments

- Speak and play the rhythm of the song using small percussion instruments
- Use greetings as ostinati on a particular instrument, e.g.,

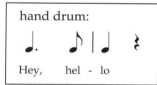

- Combine the ostinati to make a new piece
- Introduce, use, and compare instruments from different countries
- Accompany the song with the bass line (F C F C) in half notes
- Accompany the song in half notes, using the triads of F (F A C) and C (C E G) or C7 (C E G B♭); small children could play two alternating notes: F C or A G or F E or just C; older children could play alternating thirds: F&A, G&B♭
- Divide into two groups, one group playing the chord F A C and the other the chord C E G
- Discover patterns using the notes of the two chords

Play materials

- e.g., chiffon scarves, wooden spoons, stones, pinecones, wooden spinning tops, balls
- Find ways of getting to know the material (feeling, smelling, touching, listening…)
- Find ways of greeting a partner using a particular material or two different materials
- Invent movements with the material to accompany each greeting in the song

Hey, Hello, Bonjour

Traditional

1. Hey, hel - lo, bon - jour, gu - ten Tag!

2. Wel - come, wel - come, wel - come, wel - come!

3. Bue - nos di - as, bue - nos di - as!

This song uses greetings from other countries and works well as a canon. It is easy to accompany using the chords of F major and C major, and it encourages interest in other languages and countries.

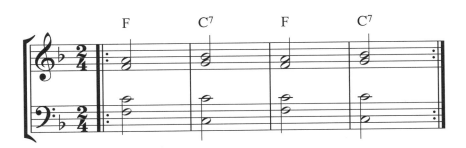

Good Morning—Extensions

Voice/Language
- Imagine you are holding a tone in your hand; carry this through the room while humming it quietly; a cluster of many different tones should result; everyone breathes independently
- Carry your tone and sing using different syllables and sustaining it as long as possible, e.g., na, ti, sew, do, lee, may
- Sing the rhythm of the song using one or more syllables
- Sing the song with different expressions, e.g., sad, excited, nervous, happy, tired
- Sing the words "Good morning" on F, A, and C to accompany the whole song
- Use other words or phrases

Movement/Dance
- Find typical gestures from different countries to accompany the words
- Sing the song using sign language
- Invent a series of gestures to accompany each line of the song with a partner; at the end of the song count or play two bars to give the children time to find a new partner; repeat the song and the gestures with many different partners
- Find dances in which the partner or group greet each other

Instruments
- Play the quarter note pulse with your hands
- Emphasize the first beat of the bar
- Play the pulse with different gestures, e.g., stamping/clapping; clapping/snapping; patting/clapping

- Make and play ostinati using body instruments or percussion; play them singly or combine them, e.g.,

- Play the melody of each phrase as an ostinato
- Using barred instruments play accompaniments on the chord of F (F A C), e.g.,

- Using barred instruments play the bass: F C F C F etc.
- Use the chords of F and C to accompany the whole song

Related subjects: Different countries and their language, music, dance, clothing, food, etc., other songs, dances, and music in ¾ meter

Good Morning

Traditional

Good morn-ing, good morn-ing, gu-ten Mor-gen, gu-ten Mor-gen, bue-nos

di-as, bue-nos di-as, buon___ gior-no, buon___ gior-no.

ossia:

The melody of this round is traditional and well known as "London's burning" or "Scotland's burning." Here it can use one or many languages and, if accompanied, it can use one chord (F major) or two chords (F and C Major).

Original text: London's burning, London's burning,
fetch the engines, fetch the engines.
Fire, fire, fire, fire,
pour on water, pour on water.

Weather text: Look it's raining, look it's raining,
thunder's calling, thunder's calling,
lightning strikes, lightning strikes,
and the storm is now over.

Inner Anner Oo—Extensions

Movement

- Choose short/long movements or gestures for each word or phrase
- Enlarge these movements so that they take you away from your spot into the room
- Invent a clapping game with a partner
- Learn the words and their rhythm – in a small group invent movements to form a dance

Language/Voice

- Invent new endings instead of "me and you" to rhyme with "too" e.g., "just a few"
- Work with one vowel, changing the syllables while keeping the rhythm, e.g., with "a":

    Annnar annar aaa, cappar tannar taa

    Zatta valla, zatta valla, ma and ya

- Invent new nonsense words to fit the rhythm
- Invent a new rhyme with a different rhythm
- Chant the rhyme in canon—with or without movements

Body-Instruments

- Clap or pat the beat while reciting the words
- Walk (and clap) to the beat while reciting the words
- Clap the rhythm of the words, making a movement to show the pause
- Walk to the beat while clapping and speaking the words

Listening

- One child speaks the rhyme with a particular emotion (happy, sad, angry...); his/her partner imitates the way of speaking; experiment with many different emotions/feelings and swap roles
- One child sings the first phrase freely; his/her partner listens and repeats, etc.; swap roles
- The teacher sings each phrase using, for example, the pitches D and A, the group repeats
- Extend the range, e.g., D E F G A; the teacher (or a child) sings a phrase, the group repeats
- Working in pairs, one child sings one phrase of the rhyme using the notes D to A, the partner repeats the melody, etc.; swap roles to invent new melodies.
- In pairs, take turns singing each phrase; play these phrases on an instrument, e.g., recorder, xylophone

Social forms

- Play a simple clapping accompaniment with a partner: 1st beat—clap your own hands, 2nd beat—clap against your partner's hands
- Invent variations with your partner, e.g., one hand, crossing hands, etc.; show the pattern to the group

Inner Anner Oo

Traditional Playground

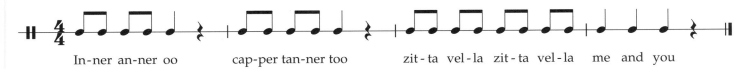

In-ner an-ner oo   cap-per tan-ner too   zit-ta vel-la zit-ta vel-la   me and you

Origin

I have lived in Graz, Austria for many years and worked in many institutions including an integrated kindergarten with hearing and hearing-impaired children, which my daughter also attended. I heard this rhyme from her; she had learned it on the playground. This is an English version. In German it would be written: "Inne anne u, kappa tanna tu, zitterwelle, zitterwelle, Dran bist du."

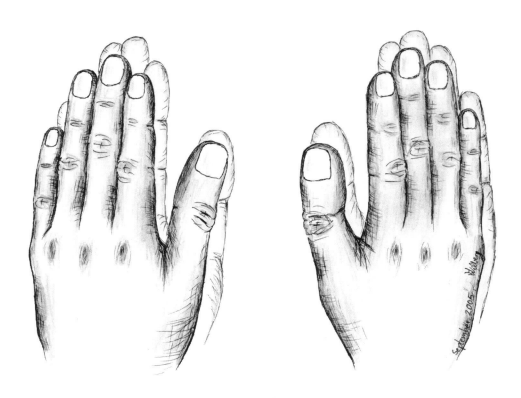

Drama

- Interpret the story that the rhyme tells; there may be many versions
- Tell the story in pantomime (without speaking)

Related subjects

- Different countries: learn rhymes from different countries whose languages you don't yet know

Dum Dum Daya—Extensions

Instruments

- Accompany rhyme or song with beat or ♩ ♩ ♩ 𝄽
- Use one or two fingers or other body instruments instead of clapping
- Transfer the clapping pattern to mallets
- Transfer the clapping pattern to percussion instruments, e.g., claves, hand drums, finding ways of producing different sounds
- Clap or accompany on the offbeats
- Use barred instruments and the notes C D E G A, e.g., play on the 1st and 3rd beats; play on the offbeats; invent a short ostinato to accompany the piece; play a bordun on C and G (on the first beat) throughout

Voice

- Use different qualities (e.g., whispering)
- Accents (on "dum")
- Leave words out without losing time, e.g., daya, kaya, me acka
- Increase the words you leave out
- Divide into two groups and speak or sing alternate phrases

Social forms

- Learn the pattern in a circle, building on one element at a time
- Play the pattern with a partner in own time
- Play the pattern with a partner in given time for the whole group
- During the last phrase look for a new partner
- Two circles, moving around to a new partner on the last phrase

Drama

- Use the rhyme for different situations, and alter tempo, movements, and language
- Invent a story where the rhyme/song plays a part

Dum Dum Daya

Traditional Playground

Dum dum day - a, Dum___ dum a - way - a way - a, Sis - si kay - a sis -

- si a - way - a way - a, Ma - ma me ac - ka, ma - ma me ay - a, Ma - ma me ac - ka,

ma - ma me ay - a, Ooc - ka pac - ka ooc - ka pac - ka ooc - ka pac - ka, Stomp!

My daughter brought this game back from a camp. Since then I have used it in many forms and with many different age groups. It is fun to sing, especially with the syncopation and good for coordination. It is interesting to try the clapping pattern with different partners.

Stand facing your partner. The pattern repeats throughout the song. All claps are on the beat.

1st measure, beats 1 and 2: with the left hands facing up and right hands facing down, clap on your partner's hands twice

1st measure, beats 3 and 4: both hands vertical facing your partner, clap on partner's hands twice

2nd measure, beats 1 and 2: clap your own hands together twice

2nd measure, beats 3 and 4: keep your hands in front of you and shake twice in the air

Omotchio—Extensions

Sensory awareness

- Use different movements on one's own body for each phrase, e.g.,
  1st phrase: clapping rhythm up and down on one arm and then on the other arm
  2nd phrase: clapping with both hands, varying the sound (high, low, loud, soft)
  3rd phrase: stroking parts of the legs strongly and rhythmically to the beat
  4th phrase: play the pitches (low, middle, high) on your torso
- Do the movements with your eyes closed
- Preparation for the following idea: stand or sit behind your partner, place your hands on his/her back, stroke lightly, massage, use different parts of your hands (knuckles, palm, edge…) to explore and get to know your partner's back and shoulders and discover the size
- Play the different phrases of the rhyme on your partner's back, inventing your own variations; spend time afterwards listening to your partner tell you what he experienced; swap roles

Movement

- Walk around the room to a beat and clap in time as in the first phrase: first in the middle and then at eye-level
- Play the second phrase on you body: "Pet" = clap; "tan" = gently tap any part of your body; "ko" = clap
- Play the second phrase by clapping and at "tan" gently tapping on other children's shoulders or back
- Invent different types of movement for each phrase, e.g., 1st phrase clapping, 2nd phrase hopping, 3rd phrase turning, 4th phrase striding

Language

- Learn individual words using an echo game (without divulging the theme of the game)
- Learn one phrase at a time and vary the call by using different dynamics (loud, soft, crescendo, decrescendo), different emotions (happy, sad, nervous, curious….), and different vocal qualities (speaking, whispering, reciting….)
- In four groups, each group speaks one phrase; each group speaks the whole rhyme as a canon
- Decide with a partner what one phrase could mean
- Collect ideas for each phrase and invent a story around the words

Instruments

- Transfer the rhythm of each phrase to particular rhythm instruments
- In four groups, each group plays one phrase as an ostinato—build up the ostinati one at a time
- Use barred instruments (resonator bells, xylophones, glockenspiels) and play the rhythms on one note (D), on two notes (D & A) or three notes (D F♯ A)
- Play a bordun on D and A while chanting the rhyme
- Invent ostinati on D F♯ A – play them to accompany the rhyme
- Use the (popular Japanese) scale D E F A B♭; improvise or compose a melody for the words

Omotchio

Japan: Traditional

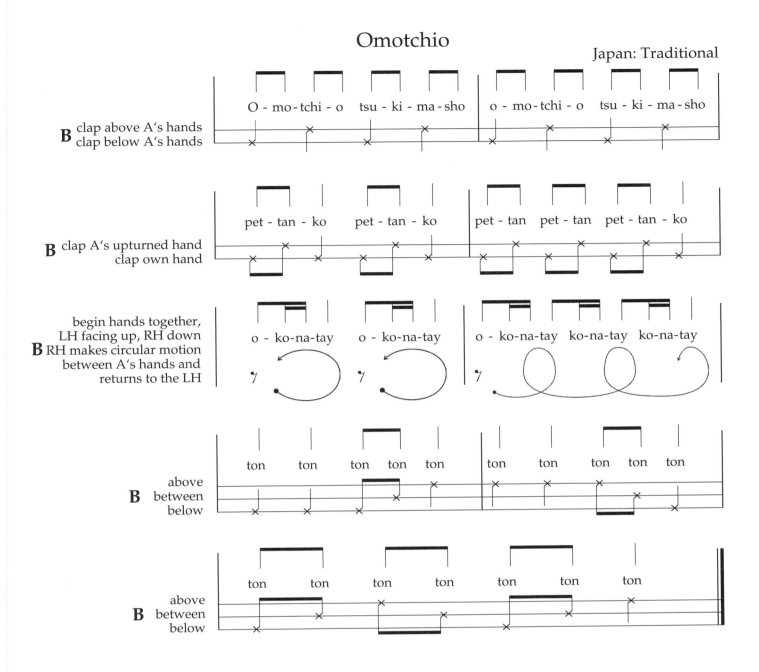

Game: This is an authentic Japanese Children's clapping game that I first learned from Doug Goodkin. Later I talked to Japanese students who explained the text, corrected my pronunciation and showed me variations. The theme of the game is making pastry. "Omotchio" refers to eating, "tsukimasho" to beating the dough. "Pettanko" is the sound of the beating and "Okonatay" is the kneading. "Ton ton…" is sung on the first, fifth and octave, e.g., D A D'.

Easy version: Everybody does the movements.
Authentic version: The first child (A) stretches out one hand with the palm face up. The hand stays still. The other hand claps the beat vertically. The second child (B) stands opposite and does the movements to the clapping game.
Line 1: B claps in time below and above A's hands.
Line 2: B claps the syllable "TAN" on the up-turned hand of A, other syllables on own hand.
Line 3: B makes a flat circular movement between A's hands; LH remains still.
Lines 4 and 5: B claps below, between and above according to the pitches.

The River is Flowing—Extensions

Sensory awareness

- Find different movements on your own body to represent raindrops, hail, waterfall, and waves; play these on your arms, shoulders, legs, etc.
- Stand or sit behind your partner; get to know his/her back by gently massaging using different parts of your hand and different types of movements while also varying the pressure
- Play different types of water on your partner's back, e.g., raindrops, hail, waterfall, waves
- Swap roles and afterwards tell each other what you experienced

Listening

- Listen to recordings of natural sounds of water (drops, rain, waves….); accompany these with your own movements
- Draw or paint a small picture or symbol for each type of water that you hear
- Find pieces combining natural sounds with instruments
- Listen to parts of pieces on themes related to water, e.g., *The Moldau* (Smetena); *La Mer* (Debussy); find out what the composer's ideas were
- Look for songs with an aspect of water as their theme, e.g., "Raindrops Keep Falling on My Head"

Instruments

- Experiment with percussion instruments, e.g., drums, shakers, maracas, triangles, cabasa, to create different types of water sounds (rain, snow, waves….); vary tempo and dynamics; decide on an order for the sounds, also using repetition
- Use instruments, e.g., drums, rain sticks, ocean drum, to create an introduction and background of water noises for the song
- Speak and play ostinati

- Play these ostinati using body instruments or percussion instruments, singly or superimpose them; make an introduction using some or all of the ostinati and use them to accompany the song
- Use barred instruments (resonator bells, xylophones, glockenspiels, metallophones) to play an accompaniment adapting the complexity to suit the abilities of the children

Play materials

- Choose one of a selection of colored chiffon scarves (white, grey, different shades of blue) and find different flowing movements with it; vary the levels (high, middle, low) and the speed
- Let each child show one of his/her ideas for the other children to imitate
- Working in pairs, find flowing movements together—side by side or as a mirror, find variations to include very small and also very large movements
- Find a large sheet, e.g., made of parachute material, and stand so that it is stretched and all the children are holding an edge of it; find gentle and stronger flowing movements, vary the tempo and height, make a small composition using these ideas

The River is Flowing

Traditional

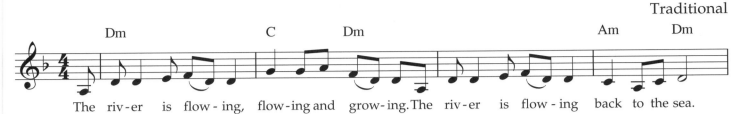

The riv-er   is   flow - ing,   flow-ing and   grow-ing. The   riv -er   is   flow - ing   back   to   the   sea.

Moth-er   is carry-ing me   child   I will al-ways be.   Moth-er   is carry-ing me   back   to   the   sea.

There are a few versions of this song with slight changes to the words and melody.
Syncopation plays a part in this version. The chords of D minor, C major, and A
minor are playable on diatonic barred instruments.

Visualizing

- Use pictures of water in different forms (raindrops, clouds, waterfall, ice, snow,
  sea….) as impulses for movement, sounds, and words
- Use cards with symbols to represent different types of water and their sounds,
  e.g.,

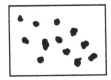  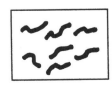  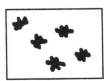

Canoe Round—Extensions

Sensory awareness

- Listen to the melody with you eyes open, then closed
- The melody moves around the room—hear where it is at the end
- Without the melody try out different positions to rock in, e.g., standing, sitting, kneeling
- Join hands with a partner and experiment with rocking, moving in time with each other
- Stand or sit back to back and experiment with rocking
- Alone or with a partner vary the tempo and the dynamics

Movement

- Listen to the melody, move through the room and stand still when the melody finishes
- Repeat and make a special statue at the end of the melody
- Change direction at the end of a phrase when the song is repeated
- Move together with a partner—side by side or behind one another
- Find movements representing paddling or rowing
- Choose one movement/gesture to accompany each line
- Play movements while imagining the song
- Sing the song as a round accompanied by the movements

Instruments

- Play the beat using body instruments: ♩ or ♪
- Clap the rhythm of the song
- Combine the beat with the rhythm of the song
- Use percussion instruments for the beat and rhythm
- Add the bass (D) and the notes of the D minor triad (D F A)
- Sing or play the last two bars as an introduction and accompaniment
- Take parts of the text as ostinati, e.g.,

Drama

- Read the book *Little Beaver and the Echo* by Amy MacDonald (text) and Sarah Fox-Davies (illustrations), Walker Books Ltd., London, 1990
- Find instruments and sounds to represent the different animals (young beaver, old beaver, duck, otter, turtle), the canoe, and the water
- Let the children take over the speaking roles of the animals
- Let the children sing the animals' questions and replies spontaneously
- Use the melody of the "Canoe Round" to represent traveling by boat

Play materials

- Objects that float
- Objects that can make movement to represent the water, the waves,
- Objects that can be used as boats

Related topics

- Echoes in sound and movement; friendship; boats; travel

Canoe Round

Canada: Traditional

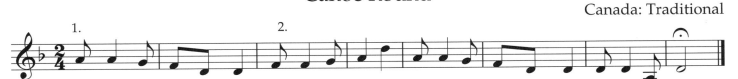

1. My pad-dle's keen and bright, flash-ing with sil-ver, Fol-low the wild goose flight. Dip, dip and swing.
2. Dip, dip and swing her back, flash-ing with sli-ver, Swift as the wild goose flies. Dip, dip and swing.

This two-part round from Canada is in D minor and can be accompanied using the notes of the triad. It has a lovely swing to it and gives many impulses for movement, drama, and work with instruments.

The Seasons—Extensions

Sensory awareness
- Choose objects related to different seasons, e.g., pinecones, leaves, flowers
- Feel these objects with closed eyes
- Try and recognize them
- Listen to sounds from nature, e.g., rain, waterfall, waves, wind, thunder

Movement
- Experiment with movements for each verse (e.g., falling leaves, dancing snowflakes, growing bulbs, flying mosquitoes)
- Change the height, direction, tempo, and dynamics of the movements
- Accompany the movements with your voice or with simple instruments

Dance
- Experiment with different steps; choose which steps fit each part of the song
- Find a simple dance form in a circle for the refrain
- Experiment and choose movements for each verse
- Incorporate, e.g., colored scarves, using different color groups for each verse

Voice and language
- Find vocal sounds for a sound-picture for each verse (during, before, or afterwards)
- Extend the refrain, e.g., "come and clap/stamp with me"
- Using suggestions from the children, extend each season by inventing two or more new verses
- Write about your favorite season

Instruments
- Experiment and find sounds to represent parts of the song (e.g., leaves falling, snowflakes dancing)
- Accompany the song clapping, stamping, and patting the beat
- Learn rhythmic ostinati to accompany the song, e.g., "meadow"; "come and play with me"
- Use body instruments then small percussion instruments
- Use a bordun on D and A throughout the piece (using no harmonic progressions)
- Using barred instruments play the notes D, F, and A on the beat, on every other beat, or an ostinato using words, e.g., "meadow," "play with me," "over in the meadow"

Listening to music
- Choose short parts of Vivaldi's *The Four Seasons*
- Practice listening to short excerpts relaxed and with eyes closed
- Concentrate on individual associations
- Listen and "conduct" the flow of the music (eyes closed)
- "Paint" the music with hands, feet, etc.
- "Paint" the music on your partner's back
- With older children, listen to particular musical events, e.g., dynamics, types of instruments, solo-tutti, pitch; express these in movement and/or on paper

The Seasons

Text: Shirley Salmon

Gerda Bächli

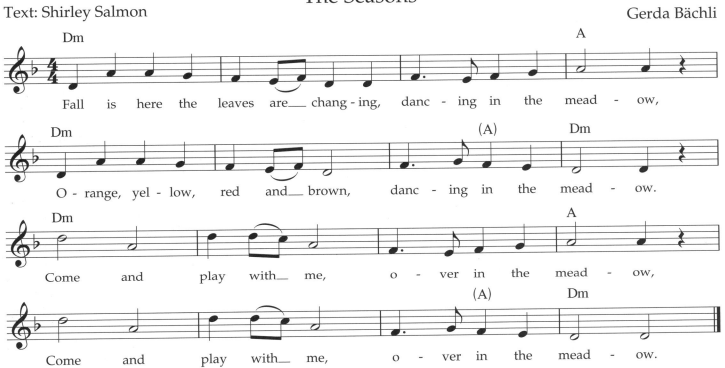

Fall is here the leaves are changing,
dancing in the meadow,
Orange, yellow, red and brown,
dancing in the meadow.

Come and play with me,
over in the meadow,
Come and play with me,
over in the meadow.

Fall is here the leaves are changing
 Dancing in the meadow.
Orange, yellow, red and brown
 Dancing in the meadow.

Winter's here and snow is falling
 Over in the meadow.
Snowflakes swirling shining white
 Over in the meadow.

Come and play with me
 Over in the meadow.
Come and play with me
 Over in the meadow.

Spring is here and plants awakening
 Over in the meadow.
Leaves and petals slowly growing
 Over in the meadow.

Summer's here the sun is shining
 Over in the meadow.
Children dancing, playing, skipping
 Over in the meadow.

23

Noah—Extensions

Movement

- Find different hand movements for each animal
- Explore movements for one animal in different situations, e.g., playing, hunting, feeding
- Extend these movements by varying the tempo, the strength, the space
- Contrast the movements of different animals with a partner
- Explore Rudolf von Laban's basic body movements: rotation, elevation, locomotion, position and gesture, generally, and also in association with particular animals

Language

- Sing the song together
- Choose different animals and their noises for the last part of the song, e.g., cow–moo; pig–oink; cat–miaow; dog–woof
- Change the words to ask about activities of the particular animal, e.g., I'm a bird and I can fly
- Let a child sing the part of Noah and two children sing as a pair of animals
- Take individual animals and speak their names rhythmically; discover which animals have the same rhythm
- Make ostinati out of animals' names with or without body instruments; repeat them singly or combine them, e.g.,

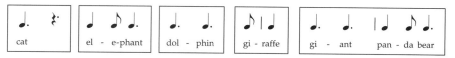

Listening

- Listen to recordings of natural sounds, e.g., weather, different types of water
- Make and listen to recordings of different environments, e.g., in town, in the playground, in the park
- Listen to recordings of different types of animals
- Find out what noises a hippo, a rhino, a dolphin and other animals make, learn to recognize them
- Listen to and sing songs about animals
- Listen to whole or parts of pieces about animals; some have a story: *Peter and the Wolf* (Prokofiev), *Flight of the Bumble Bee* (especially the recording by Bobby McFerrin), *The Carnival of the Animals* (Saint Säens), *The Firebird* (Stravinsky)

Instruments

- Play on the first beat of each measure
- Play dotted quarter notes
- Play the rhythm of the song
- Choose instruments to play
  1. The first part of the story
  2. Noah's line ("Who goes there and what can you do
  3. The answer of the particular animal
- Accompany using the bass notes of the chords D, G, and A playing ♩. or ♩.

Noah

Shirley Salmon

No - ah built his ark of wood wide and long.____ With room for all the
an - i - mals weak and strong. "Who goes there?____ And what can__ you
do"?____ "I'm a mouse:____ squeak squeak squeak."
ossia: "please let me in."

Related topics: The story of Noah's arc; information about animals
and their habitats; animals in visual art; animals in different religions

Incy Wincy Spider—Extensions

Sensory awareness

- Make finger movements imitating a spider
- Let the spider crawl on different parts of your body
- Copy or find gestures to accompany all parts of the song
- Use these movements to tell the story on your partner's back
- Feel webs made of different materials (string, wool, plastic…)
- Balance on a web made of sticky tape on the floor; try out different movements

Movement/Dance

- Learn the finger play; tell the story with your fingers
- Share the roles with a partner and tell the story with your hands
- Find movements for the spider, the rain, and the sun using different parts of the body
- Represent the spider, the sun, and rain as a group
- Find movements for a dance to go with the song

Instruments

- Use instruments (body instruments, home-made instruments, classroom instruments) to represent the spider, rain, and sun and join in at the right places in the song
- Make a piece in a small group using these sounds but without the song
- Rehearse, perform and record the pieces; listen to them again and find ways of improving them
- Find ways of notating these pieces
- Use rhythm instruments to play the beat and the rhythm of the words
- Play ostinati based on the text, e.g., Up the water spout, Incy Wincy

Language

- Use gestures to illustrate words; use words in a different context, e.g., movement words: up, down, out; nouns: spider, water spout, rain, sunshine; verbs: climb up, come down, dry
- Continue the story in your own words (with or without rhyming)
- Use the rhythm of the song and invent a story about a different animal
- Read Eric Carle's story, *The Very Busy Spider*; imitate the noises of the animals; play the story with instruments.

Play materials

- Create webs out of different materials (e.g., string, wool, plastic threads) stuck on different backgrounds (e.g., paper, cardboard, wood)
- Create webs on the floor that can be balanced upon (e.g., with tape)
- Create a flexible web made of a large ball of trouser-elastic: each child in the large circle holds one or two strands of the web; the web can move (with or without music) in many different ways
- Let a child be a "spider" and move in and out of parts of the moving web

Listening

- Listen to recordings of different types of rain; make your own recordings.
- Imitate the natural sounds with your voice or instruments

Incy Wincy Spider

Traditional

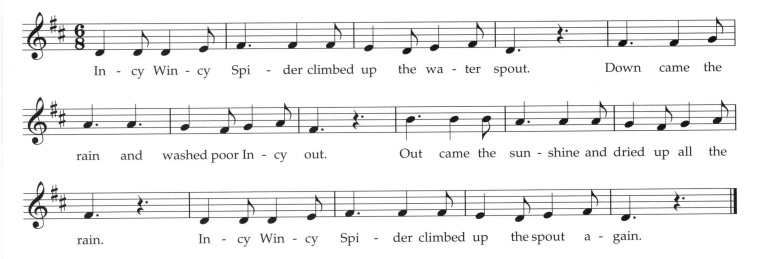

In - cy Win - cy Spi - der climbed up the wa - ter spout. Down came the

rain and washed poor In - cy out. Out came the sun - shine and dried up all the

rain. In - cy Win - cy Spi - der climbed up the spout a - gain.

Play form

Phrase 1: Use the fingers of both hands to represent a spider climbing up;

- or use one hand as a spider climbing up the other arm;
- or climb up using a thumb and the index finger of the other hand, swinging around to use the other thumb with the other index finger, etc.

Phrase 2: Raise both hands and lower them slowly wriggling the fingers to make the rain.

Phrase 3: Make the sun by drawing a big circle with both arms and hands.

Phrase 4: Climb up as in the first line.

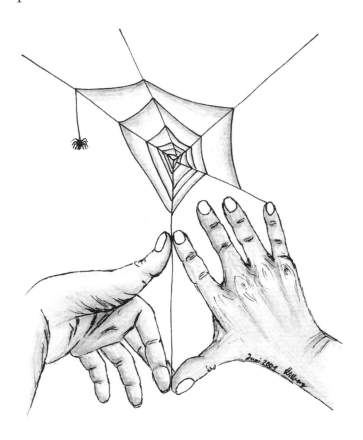

The Frogs—Extensions

Movement

- Using different body instruments (clapping, patting, etc.), play the beat
- Play the first and third beats and have other children play the second and fourth beats with a contrasting sound
- For younger children and as preparation for the clapping game, learn individual elements to accompany the song on the beat, e.g., hands together swing from left to right and back again and clap twice
- Try this standing in front of a partner, clapping the last two beats on your partner's hands, e.g., hands together in front of the body, the left hand staying still: the right hand claps on own left hand, then above with the partner's right hand, then own hand, then claps the partner's hand underneath; e.g., reverse this pattern keeping the right hand still
- Using these elements (and others), let the pairs invent their own ostinato to accompany the song

Voice

- Think of different environments and change the words accordingly, e.g., over in the desert; up in the mountain; in the big city
- Sing the song as a round
- Use individual phrases as ostinati to accompany the song, e.g., "Down by the river"; "they all stand up"; "H E double L O"

Instruments

- Using different body instruments (clapping, patting, etc.) play the beat
- Choose small percussion instruments and play: the beat / the off beat
- Let one group of instruments play the first and third beats and another group play the second and fourth beats using contrasting sounds
- Practice individual phrases, enjoying the syncopation, e.g.,

- Use barred instruments with the notes C, D, E, G, A and C'
- Play a bordun on C and G in the bass and other combinations above on the first and third beats

Listening

- Going around the circle let each child clap once – listen to the different qualities
- Repeat the task making the claps as different as possible
- Repeat with your eyes closed
- Listen to and watch clapping games from different societies
- Listen to music involving body percussion, e.g., Spanish flamenco, Austrian Schuhblattler, an extract from the piece *Clapping* by Steve Reich

The Frogs

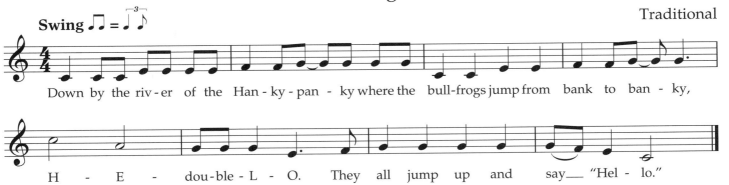

Down by the riv-er of the Han-ky-pan-ky where the bull-frogs jump from bank to ban-ky,

H - E - dou-ble-L - O. They all jump up and say___ "Hel - lo."

This is another song I learned from a friend's daughter in England. The movements of the two children are symmetrical but change levels, sometimes meeting the hand of the partner and sometimes making sounds on one's own body.

Clapping Game (for older children)

Starting position: Hands together vertically in front of the body, elbows bent. All the movements are on the quarter note beats. The pattern has two measures that are repeated four times, the last time being shortened by the handshake.

Measures 1, 3, 5, 7

Beats 1 and 2: Keeping the hands together, swing from left to right and then back, just touching the finger tips of your partner as you pass.

Beats 3 and 4: Hands together in front of the body, left hand remains still: right hand claps on own left hand, and then above on the right hand of your partner.

Measures 2, 4, 6

Beats 1 and 2: Right hand claps on own left hand, then underneath on the right hand of one's partner.

Beats 3 and 4: Left hand slaps own left thigh, then snap right-hand fingers.

Ending (Measure 8)

At "Hello" shake right hands with your partner.

Social forms

- Learn one ostinato with the whole group; let the pairs practice silently in their own tempo and gradually add the words and melody until everyone is sure of the movements
- Practice with your eyes closed
- After the song, count one empty bar giving time to quickly find a new partner to start the song again on time

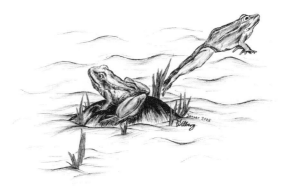

The Owl—Extensions

Movement

- Listen to the melody (without the words), then while listening again "paint" the melody in the air with one and then the other hand
- Use both hands to make parallel or mirror movements
- When the melody is played fly away from your nest or house moving around the room; arrive home before the melody has finished
- Make a journey with a partner, one flying in front of the other; change roles

Instruments

- Choose an instrument to represent the clock that will strike, e.g., triangle, cymbal; the child playing the clock decides how late it is and, at the end of the song, plays the right number of chimes
- Place a selection of instruments in the middle of the circle to represent the "night music" or the "music of the wood"; one child is chosen as the owl; once the song is finished he/she flies around the circle to the sound of the chimes, choosing musicians by touching them lightly on the shoulder
- The musicians go to the instruments in the middle of the circle and improvise on a theme e.g., "night" or "wood"; when they have finished, the roles of the owl and clock are chosen anew
- Accompany the song using E minor alternating with D major

Social forms

- Choose a partner and decide who is going to be "blind"; the seeing partner leads the blind partner around the room
- Lead a "blind" partner by playing a resonator bell or by using your voice

Listening

- With a partner choose one resonator bell and mallet; the first child closes his/her eyes, stands still and listens to his partner playing occasionally while moving around the room; when the sounds stop, the first child looks to see whether he heard where his/her partner had stopped
- Place a range of resonator bells and mallets spaced out on the floor; let the children visit the resonator bells, playing and listening (this can be a particular scale or triad but doesn't have to be)
- Each child chooses one resonator bell and mallet to represent a house
- One child flies around the room as an "owl," visiting the houses and listening to their sounds; when the owl is near, the house sounds; let two owls fly
- One child closes his eyes and moves around the "magical wood"; when he/she is near a tree (resonator bell), it sounds, warning him/her; if the child is in danger or is moving out of the wood, all the trees play

Visualizing

- Listen to the number of times the clock bell chimes and find ways of notating them
- Use cards with notation for the number of chimes
- Let the owl fly to different houses in the room – each house being played by a different type of instrument; draw the route of the owl and the sounds it heard

The Owl

Text: Shirley Salmon

Gerda Bächli

In the night the church bells sound. And the owl flies through the town.

Come to me, let me play, when it's (5) o'-clock.

Possible accompaniment:

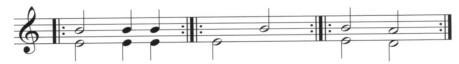

This song was written (originally in German) by Gerda Bächli, who has written many wonderful songs for and with children of all ages. The idea of an owl flying to different church towers came from Gertrud Orff. In my version there are many possibilities for the owl, e.g., to visit different trees, clock towers, or listen to an improvised "night music." The children can take over different roles, e.g., the owl, the bell chiming the hour, or the music of the trees.

Related topics: Animals that see at night; chimes of different bells

Piippu—Extensions

Sensory awareness

- Sing the melody without the words, listen with eyes closed
- Listen in different positions—sitting, lying, standing, kneeling
- Sway gently to the melody while keeping your eyes closed
- In a comfortable position sway individual parts of the body, e.g., hand, arm, upper body
- Work with a partner: stand/sit behind your partner and gently rock him/her in time; change roles
- With a partner, sit/stand facing each other, join hands, sway together in time

Play materials

- Use a soft material, e.g., chiffon scarves or long silk bands to move to the beat
- Experiment with and combine different levels (high, middle, low)
- Use the space around you: in front, at the side, behind
- Use the movements with the material to take you during the song from one spot to another far away

Instruments

- Imagine a big drum in front of you and practice playing the beat in the air one hand at a time
- Work with the chime bars of the D minor chord (D F A) in more than one octave if possible; the children have one chime bar each; accompany the song spontaneously
- Play the notes of the D minor chord only on the beat
- Using two of the notes, play the lower one on the first beat and the higher one on the second and third beats
- Learn ostinati—using syllables from the song; play the ostinati individually or play an introduction bringing in one ostinato at a time; accompany the song using all the ostinati

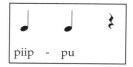  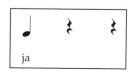 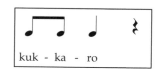

- Learn all or part of the melody on a barred instrument
- Learn a second voice:

- Learn to hear and play the harmony of the song using the bass notes: D D D D A D A D (played in dotted half notes)
- Have two groups, one playing the D minor chord (D F A) and one playing the A7 chord (A C♯ E G); conduct the groups; later let the children play without a conductor
- Play the harmonies on barred instruments, e.g., bass notes

Piippu

Finland: Traditional

Piip - pu piip - pu kuk - ka - ro ja piip - pu

kuk - ka - ro ja kuk - ka - ro ja kuk - ka - ro ja piip - pu.

This is a traditional Finnish song with a simplified version of the words involving a pipe (piippu) and (ja) a purse (kukkaro). The original story is humorous and says that a pipe and a purse are the only furniture (mööpeleitä) that a confirmed bachelor (vanhanpojan) has. The second verse tells us that a pail or bowl (kiulu) and a bucket (ämpäri) are the only furniture that an old maid (vanhan piian) needs. Because the pronunciation is not easy, I prefer the simplified text (above).

1. Piippu, piippu, kukkaro ja piippu,
   Vanhanpojan mööpeleitä: kukkaro ja piippu.

2. Kiulu, kiulu, ämpäri ja kiulu,
   Vanhan piian mööpeleitä: ämpäri ja kiulu.

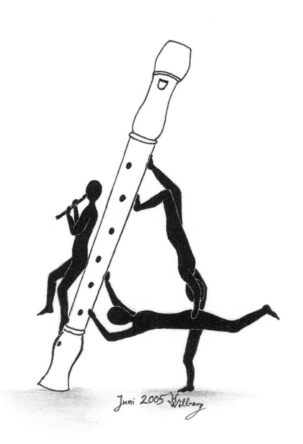

Bajuschki Baju—Extensions

Instruments
- Rock gently in time with the half beats
- Pat the half beats
- Clap the rhythm of the song
- Clap or play an ostinato
- Accompany the song playing D then A as half notes
- Use barred instruments to play the triad of D minor (D F A) and A7 (A C♯ E G) changing every half note
- Accompany on the piano or guitar using the chords D minor, A7, F, and C
- Learn the introduction on barred instruments or recorder

Sensory awareness, language, and movement
- Use the positions mentioned in the following poem
- Find new positions alone or with a partner
- Listen to the poem and imagine the sounds
- Try to create these sounds quietly using your voice or body instruments
- Accompany the poem with movements
- Invent new verses

Listening Poem[1]

If you lie near a window pane
You may hear the sound of rain
If you are sitting by a stream
You may hear how fishes swim
If you are still and give glance
You may hear how fireflies dance
If you are looking at the sky
You may hear just how birds fly
If you are kneeling in the grass
You may hear a squirrel pass
If you walk and come to stop
You may hear a rabbit hop
If I'm quiet and you are too
We may just hear something new

—SHIRLEY SALMON

Drama
- Read the book: *Who's That Knocking at My Door?* (by Tilde Michels and Reinhard Michl) and enjoy the beautiful drawings
- Use a narrator and play the story in pantomime
- Use instruments to represent the different animals
- Let the children speak the dialogues
- Sing the dialogues spontaneously

Related topics

Lullabies from different countries; Russian music and fairy tales

1 Based on the idea of the poem "Das leise Gedicht" by Alfred Könner

Bajuschki Baju
(Bī´-yüsch-kē Bī-yü´)

This flowing Russian lullaby has a soft melancholy feeling about it. It can be accompanied using two chords (D minor and A7) changing every half note or using four chords (D minor, A7, F, and C). The introduction can also be used as an intermezzo. The song can be sung in unison and parts can be added with voice or instruments according to the children's abilities.

Russian: Traditional
Accompaniment: Shirley Salmon

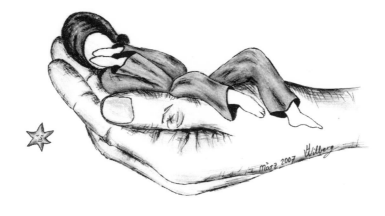

2. Fairy stories I will sing you, bajuschki baju
   Close your eyes and listen gently, bajuschki baju

3. In the dark the riders call bajuschki baju
   Sleep and ride on through the night, bajuschki baju

4. Sleep my child and dream your dreams, bajuschki baju
   Travel thousands rooms of night, bajuschki baju

5. Dream my child while others sleep, bajuschki baju
   As a ship sleeps on the water, bajuschki

The Mirror—Extensions

Movement and dance

- Let your hand or finger draw the melody in the air
- Use both hands; they can draw alternately or together
- Let your hands mirror each other
- Find a partner and mirror movement: of one part of the body, staying in one place, using the space around you, finding different shapes
- Change roles at the end of the song or at the end of each phrase
- Use a longer recorded piece of music and try to swap the roles of leading and mirroring a few times without speaking and without stopping the flow of the movements

Language

- Speak the words rhythmically
- Sing the melody using one syllable; using syllables starting with the same letter, e.g., ba, bu, bu, be, bo
- Find rhythmic ostinati from the text, e.g.,

 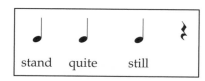 

- Try speaking and clapping them to a steady beat
- Divide into four groups: one group speaks the words of the song; the other groups speak or clap the ostinati

Social forms

- Let three children work together: one is the person in the mirror, one the child and the third holds a hoop between the two showing which part of the body is to be mirrored
- Use the idea of a shadow: try moving and sensing what is easy or difficult for your partner; change roles and discuss what you have discovered
- Use the idea of a shadow and learn a new verse:

> I've got a shadow as you can see.
> Where I go it goes with me.
> Moving fast or moving slow, the shadow is mine—
> Partner and friend in the sunshine.

- Use the idea of sun and shadow in movement improvisation

Instruments

- With a partner use body percussion for the pulse and/or ostinati; compare the different solutions
- With a partner experiment with mirroring patterns using body percussion
- Invent a pattern to accompany the whole song
- Use percussion instruments to play the pattern

The Mirror

Text: Shirley Salmon   Bolivian: Traditional

You are my mir-ror and stay quite still while I___ go just__ where I will.

But when I stop be-fore you look care-ful-ly: you must do the__ same as me.

Game:

All the children stand in a circle holding hands. One child (or more if the group is very large) walks in a circle in the middle while the group walks in the opposite direction while singing the song. At the end of the song the child in the middle stops in front of another child in the outer circle who becomes a mirror. The child in the middle uses gestures and movements that are mirrored by the other child. The two try to make it look as real as possible. When finished they change places and the "mirror" becomes the child in the middle. If the group is very big have two or three children in the middle. The melody stems from the Bolivian song "Dime Maria."

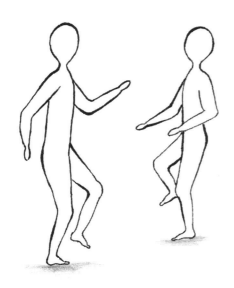

The Cobbler—Extensions

Play materials

- Thinking of the different actions a cobbler might make, find objects to imitate these sounds, e.g., use stones, shells, cones, paper…
- Order these sounds according to the actions they represent, e.g., hammering, sewing, polishing, gluing….

Instruments

- Fill the rests with two sounds using the voice or body instruments
- Using body percussion (e.g., clapping, patting, stamping) accompany the beat of the song or the rhythm of the words
- Use small percussion instruments to accompany the first part of the song, playing the rhythm of the words
- Use contrasting instruments to play during the rests and others to play the beat
- Think about the jobs a cobbler does, e.g., hammering, sewing, brushing, gluing… and choose instruments to represent the movements and sounds
- Invent a sequence of actions using these sounds, perhaps as a story; the song can be used as the recurring part of a rondo telling the story: A B A C A D, etc.
- Take the activities of the cobbler and invent ostinati for them, e.g.,

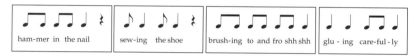

- Play these singly; experiment with different combinations; build them up (with or without speaking the words) to form an accompaniment

Visualizing

- Work with a rhythm box (or with small children just one line): the black circles are sounds and white ones are rests, e.g.,

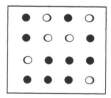

- Use the lines of the rhythm boxes as ostinati, using body percussion or instruments
- Turn, read, and play the rhythm box from each side
- Let a group of children stand on each of the four sides: each group can have a different type of instrument play each part separately and then try different combinations
- Use the voice instead—each group can choose a sound or word
- Invent your own rhythm box and find ways of notating eighth notes

Social forms

- Start with two or more percussion instruments to play the rhythms of the words of the first part of the song; it is good if there are only a few instruments, e.g., three or four for a group of ten children
- While the second part is being sung, pass the instruments clockwise; the child holding an instrument at the end of the song plays it during the first part
- Instead of passing the instruments let the children with instruments stand and move around during the second part (not playing), giving their instrument to one of the children sitting in the circle before the song starts again

The Cobbler

Text: Shirley Salmon

Traditional

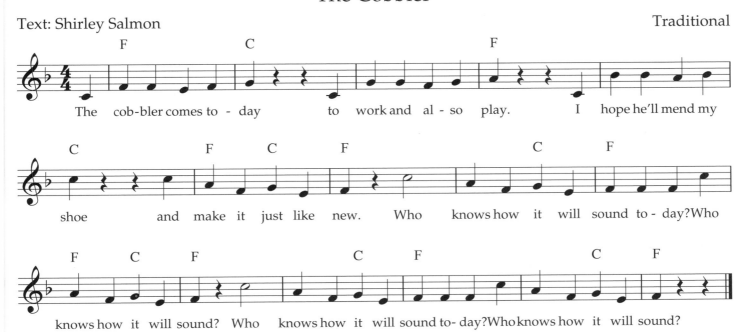

The cob-bler comes to - day to work and al - so play. I hope he'll mend my shoe and make it just like new. Who knows how it will sound to - day? Who knows how it will sound? Who knows how it will sound to- day? Who knows how it will sound?

März 2007 Willen

Related topics: Repairing things; different professions and their movements and sounds

The Drum is Going 'Round—Extensions

Sensory awareness
- Use different objects instead of drums, e.g., stones, chopsticks, spinning tops, scarves, feathers
- Make bags for the objects and feel them from the outside and inside
- Get to know your object without looking; feel the weight, shape, surface, etc.
- Feel the object on different parts of your body and your partner's body
- Use your object to join you to a partner; how can you move together?

Instruments
- Start by passing just using one drum, and then gradually add more
- Use different sorts of instruments (and change the words accordingly), e.g., shakers, bells
- Use a combination of different types of instruments
- Use different sorts of drums, e.g., from different countries; how do they differ?
- Make your own drums

Listening
- Listen to different sorts of accompaniments
- Listen to the different types of instruments (especially with your eyes closed)
- Choose a partner and an instrument; lead your "blind" partner through the room by playing your instrument; change roles
- The children stand well spaced around the room, each with an instrument: They are the "musical wood"; one child moves through the wood, and when he/she is near a tree, the tree starts to play its instrument; try it with two or more children
- Set up the magical wood; let one child move through the wood without looking (blindfolded); the trees play their instruments when the child is nearby or when the child is in danger

Social forms
- During the second part of the song, the children with drums move within the circle and pass on their drums to seated children before the song starts again
- After the drums have been passed on, allow the children to improvise together and find an ending before starting the song again

The Drum is Going 'Round

Text: Shirley Salmon

Traditional

Wel-come, wel-come we are here. Wel-come, wel-come one and all. The

drum is go-ing 'round and look-ing for a friend. The drum is go-ing 'round and look-ing for a friend.

Game

Sing the first half of the song together. When the second part starts pass a drum around the circle (without playing it). When the song ends, the drum comes to a stop too. The child with the drum accompanies the first part of the song and passes it on when the second part starts. Gradually add more drums so that more children can accompany.

Februar 2004 H. Willberg

The Train—Extensions

Movement/Dance
- Visit different countries at the end of the song, e.g., bouncing land, rocking land
- Follow the locomotive and imitate his/her movements
- Let different parts of the body lead you while singing the song
- Find movements to represent a journey by train
- Visit different countries by learning a dance from each of them

Language
- Make train sounds using your mouth, voice, or body
- Sing the song using particular consonants or vowels, e.g., ti, ta, to, tu, te; mi, ma mo
- Remember words and phrases that you can hear at the railway station; find rhythms for them; speak them separately or together
- Rewrite the song using a journey by boat, plane, car …

Instruments
- Use body instruments spontaneously to accompany the song
- Learn patterns with body instruments
- Visit different groups of instruments: wood, metal, drums, wind …..
- Invent a rhythm for each wagon; layer in one wagon/rhythm at a time
- Accompany the song playing the beat, offbeat, rhythms of the words, and ostinati

Listening
- Listen to poems or stories about traveling
- Listen to recordings made at a station noticing sounds and language
- The journey takes us to different countries—listen to their instruments and music
- Listen to pieces that involve a journey, e.g., *Pacific 231* (Honnegger)

Social forms
- Take on the role of the locomotive or one of the wagons
- Work in pairs and make your own journey with your partner
- Lead your "blind" partner on a journey

Visualizing
- Draw the journey of the melody; follow it with a finger from one hand, then the other
- Find ways of drawing or painting the sounds you hear from individual instruments

Drama
- Observe and copy everyday movements involved in traveling by train
- Make up a story about a journey using pantomime
- Using the song as a rondo, invent a piece taking you to different countries

The Train

Shirley Salmon

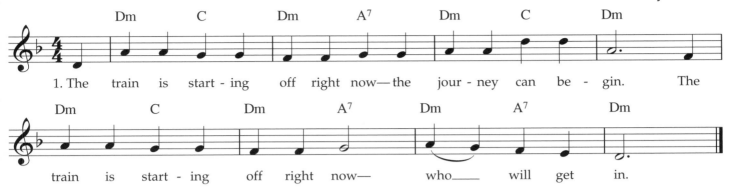

1. The train is start - ing off right now— the jour - ney can be - gin. The
train is start - ing off right now— who___ will get in.

2. The train is slowing down right now, of that there is no doubt.
   The train is slowing down right now. Who will get out?

Game

The children sit in a circle. One child is the locomotive. While everyone sings the song, the locomotive moves around the outside of the circle and stands still when the song comes to an end. The child whom he/she is standing behind becomes the new locomotive while the first child becomes one of the carriages, following the route and imitating the movements of the locomotive without holding on. Continue until all the children are in the train. In a large group it may be a good idea to start with two or three locomotives. Once all the children are in the train it's time to sing the second verse and for the children to get out of the train. This can be done by losing the last carriage first, or by naming children. Those who leave the train can join the circle and accompany the song.

My Friend—Extensions

Movement and dance

- Visit imaginary countries, e.g., bouncing land, swimming land, dwarf land, and try out typical movements
- Visit a land of letters and make the letters of the alphabet with your body—alone or with a partner, stationary or in movement
- Learn dancing steps from different countries
- Learn dances from different countries

Language

- Sing the song introducing different countries (and instruments); find them on a map
- Sing the melody using syllables starting with, e.g., t, s, b, l, c
- Sing only your own name to the melody
- Replace the words with the names of the children
- Invent nonsense words to the melody
- Learn rhymes and games from different countries and in different languages
- Find books that tell stories about children from different countries

Instruments

- Choose different countries and play their rhythms, e.g., using body percussion
- Play these rhythms on percussion instruments, introducing them one at a time over a steady beat
- Use these rhythms as ostinati to accompany the song
- Learn the bass accompaniment and find rhythmic variations to it
- Learn the accompaniments for xylophones and glockenspiels

Play materials

- Find out about costumes from different countries and draw or make similar costumes
- What games do the children play there? What toys do they have?
- Find out about games that use stones

Listening

- Listen to recordings of other languages; what can you hear? Try to imitate the sounds
- Listen to instruments from other countries; invite musicians to come and play
- Listen to music (including dances) from different countries; how can you describe it?

Related topics

- Find out about traditions from different countries
- Find out about different religions; how do they celebrate Christmas or New Year?
- What festivals do other religions have? How are they celebrated?

My Friend

Text: Shirley Salmon

C. Shartner

My friend he/she lives in Af - ri - ca, in Af - ri - ca, in Af - ri - ca;

likes to play mu - sic ev - 'ry day, let's hear him/her play

Sing the song and accompany it using body percussion. Once the song is over, one, two, or more children improvise on instruments that are typical for Africa. Next time around, let other children improvise. The instruments can also be used to accompany the song.

Hear him play

likes to play mus - ic

My friend

List of Songs and Their Extensions

Song	Page number	Sensory awareness	Movement/dance	Language/voice	Instruments	Play materials	Listening	Visualizing	Social forms	Drama
Bajuschki Baju	34	•	•	•	•					•
Canoe Round	20	•	•		•	•				•
The Cobbler	38				•	•		•	•	
The Drum is Going 'Round	40	•			•		•		•	
Dum Dum Daya	14			•	•				•	•
The Frogs	28		•	•	•		•		•	
Good Morning	10		•	•	•					
Hello Children	6	•	•	•	•					
Hey, Hello, Bonjour	8		•	•	•	•				
Incy Wincy Spider	26	•	•	•	•	•	•			
Inner Anner Oo	12		•	•	•		•		•	•
The Mirror	36		•	•	•				•	
My Friend	44		•	•	•	•	•			
Noah	24		•	•	•		•			
Omotchio	16	•	•	•	•					
The Owl	30		•		•		•	•	•	
Piippu	32	•			•	•				
The River is Flowing	18	•			•	•	•	•		
The Seasons	22	•	•	•	•		•			
The Train	42		•	•	•		•	•	•	•

About the Author

Shirley Salmon has worked with infants, children, teenagers, and adults of different abilities including those with disabilities in mainstream classes, in groups of mixed ability, in residential homes, kindergartens, and schools for more than 30 years. She studied Music at York University, England and then taught music at Ibstock Place School (the demonstration school of the Froebel Institute) London where she had been a pupil. She acquired a Post Graduate Certificate in Education from London University and, after moving to Austria, took further training in music and movement education, music therapy, sign language, and integrative education and studied educational science at the University of Innsbruck, Austria where she acquired her masters degree.

She was employed by the county of Styria, Austria from 1979–2000 using music and movement in homes for behaviourally disturbed children and teenagers and with deaf and hard-of-hearing children while also working freelance for kindergartens and schools. She has been a lecturer at the Orff-Institute in Salzburg since 1984, teaching classes in Didactics, Teaching Practicum, Theory and Practice of Music and Dance in Integrative Education and in Community Work. She coordinates the elective "Music and Dance in the Community and in Integrative Pedagogy," co-directs summer courses at the Orff-Institute, and has been director of the postgraduate university course "Advanced Studies in Music and Dance Education—Orff-Schulwerk" since 2006. She has published numerous articles in journals and has given courses, workshops, and lectures in Austria, Germany, Spain, Italy, USA, Japan, Mexico, Hungary, Denmark, Japan, and Hong Kong.

Orff-Schulwerk American Edition

MAIN VOLUMES

Music for Children 1	Pre-School	SMC 12
Music for Children 2	Primary	SMC 6
Music for Children 3	Upper Elementary	SMC 8

SUPPLEMENTARY PUBLICATIONS

AFRICAN SONGS FOR SCHOOL AND COMMUNITY
(Robert Kwami)   SMC 551
A selection of 12 songs including traditional material and original compositions by the author.

THE ANCIENT FACE OF NIGHT (Gerald Dyck)   SMC 553
A collection of original songs and instrumental pieces for SATB chorus and Orff instruments. The cycle of songs has both astronomical and musical influences. (Chorus Part: SMC 553-01)

ANIMAL CRACKER SUITE AND OTHER POEMS
(Deborah A. Imiolo-Schriver)   SMC 561
A set of four original poems arranged for speech chorus, body percussion and percussion ensemble. Twenty-one additional original poems are included for teachers and students to make their own musical settings.

ALL AROUND THE BUTTERCUP (Ruth Boshkoff)   SMC 24
These folk song arrangements are organized progressively, each new note being introduced separately.

CHIPMUNKS, CICADAS AND OWLS (Natalie Sarrazin)   SMC 552
Twelve native American children's songs from different regions.

CIRCUS RONDO (Donald Slagel)   SMC 73
A stylized circus presentation using music, movement, speech and improvisational technique, for various Orff instruments, recorders and voices.

CROCODILE AND OTHER POEMS (Ruth Pollock Hamm)   SMC 15
A collection of verses for use as choral speech within the elementary school. Included are ideas for movement, instrumental accompaniments, and proposals for related art, drama and listening activities.

DANCING SONGS (Phillip Rhodes)   SMC 35
A song cycle for voices and Orff instruments. The contemporary harmonies create a dramatic and striking experience for upper elementary/middle school grades.

DE COLORES (Virginia Ebinger)   SMC 20
Folklore from the Hispanic tradition for voices, recorders and classroom percussion.

DISCOVERING KEETMAN (Jane Frazee)   SMC 547
Rhythmic exercises and pieces for xylophone by Gunild Keetman. Selected and introduced by Jane Frazee.

DOCUM DAY (Donald Slagel)   SMC 18
An olio of songs from England, Hungary, Ireland, Jamaica, the Middle East, Newfoundland, Nova Scotia, the USA. For voices, recorders and classroom percussion.

EIGHT MINIATURES (Hermann Regner)   SMC 14
Ensemble pieces for advanced players of recorders and Orff instruments which lead directly from elementary 'Music for Children'; to chamber music for recorders.

ELEMENTAL RECORDER PLAYING
(Gunild Keetman and Minna Ronnefeld) Translation by Mary Shamrock
Teacher's Book   SMC 558
This book is based on the fundamental principles of Orff-Schulwerk. The book can be used as a foundation text in an elementary music program that includes use of the recorder. It can also be employed in teaching situations that concentrate primarily upon recorder but in which ensemble playing, improvisation and singing also play an essential role.

Student's Book   SMC 559
Includes a variety of exercises, songs, pieces, improvisation exercises, canons, duets, rondos and texts to use for making rhythms and melodies.

Student's Workbook   SMC 560
Contains exercises and games for doing at home and during the music lesson. Integrated with work in the Student's Book.

FENCE POSTS AND OTHER POEMS (Ruth Pollock Hamm)   SMC 31
Texts for melodies, 'Sound Envelopes', movement and composition written by children, selected poets and the editor. Material for creative melody making and improvisation (including jazz).

FOUR PSALM SETTINGS (Sue Ellen Page)   SMC 30
For treble voices (unison and two-part) and Orff instruments.

HAVE YOU ANY WOOL? THREE BAGS FULL! (Richard Gill)   SMC 29
17 traditional rhymes for voices and Orff instruments. Speech exercises, elaborate settings for Orff instruments using nursery rhymes to show how to play with texts.

KUKURÍKU (Miriam Samuelson)   SMC 57
Traditional Hebrew songs and dances (including Hava Nagila) arranged for voices, recorders and Orff instruments. Instructions (with diagrams) are given for the dances.

THE MAGIC FOREST (Lynn Johnson)   SMC 16
Sequenced, early childhood, music-lesson plans based on the Orff-Schulwerk approach.

PIECES AND PROCESSES (Steven Calantropio)   SMC 569
This collection of original songs, exercises, instrumental pieces, and arrangements provides fresh examples of elemental music. Along with each piece is a detailed teaching procedure designed to give music educators a collection of instructional techniques.

THE QUANGLE WANGLE'S HAT (Sara Newberry)   SMC 32
Edward Lear's delightful poem set for speaker(s), recorders and Orff instruments (with movement and dance improvisation).

¡QUIEN CANTA SU MAL ESPANTA!
Songs, Games and Dances from Latin America
(Sofia Lopez-Ibor and Verena Maschat)   SMC 568
This book presents a rich and varied selection of material from an immense geographical area, combining local traditions with foreign influences to engage and inspire teachers and students. The DVD includes demonstrations of the dances for presentation in the classroom.

THE RACCOON PHILOSOPHER
(Danai Gagne-Apostolidou and Judith Thomas-Solomon)   SMC 566
A drama in mixed meters for upper elementary grades with preparatory activities for singing, moving, playing recorder, Orff instruments and creating. The Raccoon Philosopher was inspired by thoughts on virtue by Martin Buber. As we learn from the raccoon, so we learn from the children: to be merry for no particular reason, to never for a moment be idle, and to express our needs vigorously.

RECORDERS WITH ORFF ENSEMBLE (Isabel McNeill Carley) SMC 25-27
Three books designed to fill a need for a repertoire (pentatonic and diatonic) for beginning and intermediate recorder players. Most of the pieces are intended to be both played and danced and simple accompaniments are provided.

RINGAROUND, SINGAROUND (Ruth Boshkoff)   SMC 33
Games, rhymes and folksongs for the early elementary grades, arranged in sequential order according to concepts.

ROUND THE CORNER AND AWAY WE GO (David J. Gonzol)   SMC 567
This folk song collection provides models of arrangements to be taught using Orff-Schulwerk processes. The accompanying teaching suggestions give examples of how to break down instrumental parts and sequence the presentation of them developmentally.

RRRRRO
(Polyxene Mathéy and Angelika Panagopoulos-Slavik)   SMC 79
Poetry, music and dance from Greece with Greek texts adapted for rhythmic reciting by groups accompanied by percussion and other instruments.

A SEASONAL KALEIDOSCOPE
(Joyce Coffey, Danai Gagne, Laura Koulish)   SMC 55
Original songs, poetry and stories with Orff instruments for children. Bound by a theme of seasonal changes and intended for classroom and music teachers.

SIMPLY SUNG (Mary Goetze)   SMC 23
Folk songs arranged in three parts for young singers. They include American folk songs, spirituals and Hebrew melodies.

SKETCHES IN STYLE (Carol Richards and Neil Aubrey)   SMC 19
Arrangements for classroom music. For voices, recorders and classroom percussion.

SOMETHING TOLD THE WILD GEESE (Craig Earley)   SMC 21
A collection of folksongs for unison treble voices, barred and small percussion instruments, and recorders (soprano and alto).

STREET GAMES (Gloria Fuoco-Lawson)   SMC 17
Instrumental arrangements of rhythmical hand jives based on traditional American street games.

TALES TO TELL, TALES TO PLAY
(Carol Erion and Linda Monssen)   SMC 28
Four folk tales (Indian, African, German and American Indian) retold and arranged for music and movement, with accompaniment for recorders and Orff instruments.

TEN FOLK CAROLS FOR CHRISTMAS FROM THE UNITED STATES
(Jane Frazee)   SMC 22
Settings of Appalachian and unfamiliar carols, arranged for voices, recorders and Orff instruments.

TUNES FOR YOUNG TROUBADOURS (Dianne Ladendecker)   SMC 34
Ten songs for children's voices, recorders and Orff ensemble.

WIND SONGS (Phillip Rhodes)   SMC 197
Four songs for unison voices, barred and small percussion instruments.